ROBERT B
DOMINIC RAAB

THE INSIGHT AND FASCINATING STORY OF ONE OF THE PROLONGED HAMMER-MURDER-CASE TO BE REVIEWED

GRACE PHILLIPS

TABLE OF CONTENTS

CHAPTER 1

Justice Secretary Dominic Raab agreed to consider the case of a man who killed his wife with a claw hammer during a meeting with Joanna's mother Diana Parkes and friend Hetti Barkworth-Nanton.

For the 2010 manslaughter of Joanna Simpson, British Airlines captain Robert Brown received a 26-year prison sentence.

In spite of the fact that he is scheduled for automatic release in November, Ms. Simpson's mother Diana Parkes is advocating for the case to be submitted to the parole board.

The issue was receiving Mr. Raab's "closest personal attention," he said.

In October 2010, as their two young children hid in a playroom, Brown fatally shot his 46-year-old wife in their Windsor home.

He had previously admitted manslaughter on the basis of diminished culpability before a jury at Reading Crown Court found him not guilty of murder in May 2011.

The justice secretary was "very keen on listening to what we were saying, and I believe he's going to look at it very seriously," according to Ms Parkes, who met with Mr. Raab on Thursday.

I believe he was shocked, she continued. I think we might be moving in the right direction.

During the meeting, Ms. Simpson's friend Hetti Barkworth-Nanton said: "I pressed him very hard to make guarantees, and he did expressly declare that he would surely evaluate this matter fully with his new powers."

The Secretary of State is allowed under the Police, Crime, Sentencing and Courts (PCSC) Act 2022 to submit a prisoner serving a normal determinate sentence to the parole board, which may decide whether it is safe to release them.

"He is going to complete this review under those new powers," said Ms. Barkworth-Nanton, who also serves as chair of the domestic violence advocacy group Refuge. "So we will continue to campaign for the public to put pressure on for that review to be done, and show their disgust at the situation we're in."

'Joanna Simpson was brutally killed in a heinous and despicable act that has changed the lives of her family and friends forever,' Mr. Raab said in a statement. 'I was humbled to meet with Joanna's mother and best friend today to extend my deepest sympathies for what her family has been through and to reassure her that I am giving this case my closest personal attention and will be reviewing it very carefully.'

CHAPTER 2

In December, Brown's transfer to a category D open jail was thwarted by the Prison Service.

Before being released, an airline pilot who murdered his estranged wife will go through a thorough risk assessment and may be put behind bars, activists said Tuesday.

With their two young children there, Robert Brown, 59, fatally beat his estranged wife Joanna Simpson with a claw hammer at least 14 times.

After serving 13 years of a 26-year sentence, he is eligible for automatic release this year; however, Joanna's mother Diana Parkes said she had obtained guarantees from Justice

Secretary Dominic Raab that he would undertake a thorough risk assessment of the release.

According to a law that was approved last year, Mr. Raab has the authority to send cases to the Parole Board if he believes that convicts who are about to be released might endanger the public or national security.

Apparently due to his high risk status, jail authorities prevented former British Airways pilot Brown from transferring to an open prison last year.

Mrs. Parkes, 84, begged with Mr. Raab, the victims, and the minister of sentencing, Edward Argar, to keep Brown in jail yesterday. She said that Mr. Raab, who serves as the Deputy Prime Minister, stated that Brown's release will be thoroughly risk-evaluated and called it a "significant step" in the #NotAnotherJo campaign.

Mr. Raab said that he will personally evaluate the situation following the meeting in London.

Joanna Simpson was brutally murdered in a horrible crime that, in his words, "has ruined the lives of her family and friends for life."

I had the honor of meeting with Joanna's mother and best friend to offer my sincere condolences for the hardships her family has had and to reassure her that I am giving this case my utmost personal attention and would be thoroughly analyzing it.

"My first priority is public safety. I want a lengthier sentence for serious criminals.

Carrie Johnson, the wife of former prime minister Boris Johnson, and former home secretary Priti Patel have both publicly endorsed Mrs. Parkes' candidacy.

With a hammer he had concealed in their children's school bags, Brown assaulted Joanna, 46, at their old marital home in Ascot in 2010. He then dug a hole in the woods of Windsor Great Park for her and buried her there.

The couple was embroiled in a court dispute over their money when Joanna filed for divorce following years of abuse, harassment, and intimidation.

In his court case, Brown claimed he had a "adjustment condition" brought on by stress but was cleared of murder owing to reduced responsibility.

Given his claim of lessened responsibility resulting from the condition, Mrs. Parkes questioned why he was qualified for immediate release without any medical examination. She expressed concern that he may still be a danger to her family, particularly his kids, who were just nine and 10 when their mother was slain.

At a time when the Probation Service has expressed concern about its ability to handle its current caseload, she cautioned that his release would need a high degree of surveillance.

Her close pal is Joanna. Both met Mr. Raab when Hetti Barkworth-Nanton established the Joanna Simpson Foundation in her honor.

We are grateful for the time the secretary of state and his staff spent with us, they stated in a statement sent by the foundation. We appreciate his guarantee that he would use the additional authority he now has to ask for a thorough risk assessment of Robert Brown's release. This significant growth is really encouraging to us.

When Mrs. Parkes discussed her family's concerns over Brown's release in an interview with the Daily Mail earlier this month, she expressed her gratitude for the political and public support she had received since initiating the #NotAnotherJo campaign.

Diana Parkes, the mother of Joanna Brown, is working to prevent her killer's release on parole in November after he has completed 13 of his 26-year jail term.

CHAPTER 3

Dominic Raab, the justice minister, has been requested by the family of a mother who was slain by her pilot husband in a violent assault at their house.

In October 2010, when their two small children hid in a playroom, British Airlines pilot Robert Brown fatally beat his wife Joanna with a claw hammer.

Brown put the 46-year-corpse old's in a homemade casket in Windsor Great Park after telling police that he had been "stitched up" by a prenuptial agreement.

In May 2011, a jury at Reading Crown Court found him not guilty of murder, but he was sentenced to prison anyway after earlier admitting manslaughter on the grounds of diminished responsibility.

Brown received a sentence of 24 years for manslaughter and an additional two years for impeding a coroner from doing his job.

In November, at the halfway point of his term, he is scheduled for release from jail on a license.

Diana Parkes, however, is working to halt his release because she considers it to be "nonsensical," according to Joanna.

The 83-year-old is requesting action from the justice secretary to prevent Brown's release. "Pledged to give this matter his closest personal attention," Mr. Raab said.

On Brown's release, Mrs. Parkes stated: "Our household is quite anxious.

Ad " "not only our family, but also the acquaintances of my daughter, as well as the whole public. I am concerned about any ladies he could encounter."

Ms. Parkes requested Mr. Raab's assistance by saying: "When Brown is being freed halfway through his sentence and the Probation Service is so understaffed, it is utterly absurd, and I would want him to look at our case thoroughly.

And I inquire as to who will oversee him for the duration of his 13-year license. I just don't believe the Probation Service will be able to pull this off.

According to a representative for the Ministry of Justice, "This was an atrocious crime, and our sympathies are with Joanna Simpson's family and friends.

The deputy prime minister has promised to devote his full attention to this issue and would do all in his power to keep the most dangerous criminals in jail.

People are being encouraged to write their MP and request that Brown's release be halted by the Joanna Simpsons Foundation, a charity founded in Joanna's memory.

Next week in Parliament, the charity will also conduct an event where they will introduce their campaign.

Priti Patel, a former home secretary, and Carrie Johnson, a former prime minister's wife, are among the speakers scheduled for the occasion.

In their home in Ascot, Berkshire, in October 2010, British Airways captain Robert Brown fatally beat his 46-year-old wife Joanna with a claw hammer.

The couple's two young children hid in a playroom while Brown, who thought a prenuptial agreement had "stitched him up," murdered their mother. At Windsor Great Park, he put his wife's remains inside a homemade coffin.

Brown had previously pleaded manslaughter on the basis of diminished responsibility, but a jury at Reading crown court had absolved him of murder in May 2011.

His release is scheduled for November of this year after receiving sentences of 24 years for manslaughter and an additional two years for impeding a coroner in the performance of his duties.

Diana Parkes, the 83-year-old mother of Joanna, is pleading with the justice secretary to step in because she is concerned about Brown's release from jail.

"Our family is quite anxious. not only our family, but also my daughter's friends and the whole public. I am concerned about any ladies he may encounter, she told the PA news agency.

Parkes said, "I would want him to study our case very closely and realize how totally absurd it is that Brown is being freed halfway through his sentence when the probation agency is so understaffed." This is Parkes' preferred method of appeal.

Who will oversee him over the 13 years of his license, I wonder? I really don't believe that the probation service can handle this.

At the half-term break, Brown drove to the house of his divorced wife to pick up their children. He used the hammer on her at least 14 times when the kids were out of sight.

After wrapping his wife's corpse in plastic sheets and covering her skull with a bin liner to "avoid leaving bloodstains," he tossed her body in the vehicle.

He returned with the kids to his house while driving his wife's remains to a prepared improvised casket in Windsor Great Park, which is home to the Queen.

"I just broke down. Brown said to the court at the moment, "I just explode, and that's it. "I simply blew, and the next thing I knew I was standing over Jo, and there was blood everywhere."

Later, Brown's daughter reported to the police that she had heard her parents "beating each other".

People are being urged by the Joanna Simpson Foundation to write their MP and request that Brown's release not take place.

The organization also has a campaign launch event scheduled for this week in Westminster, when it will call on the justice secretary to use his authority to prevent Brown's release.

The former justice secretary Robert Buckland, the former home secretary Priti Patel, Carrie Johnson, and Joanna's friend Hetti Barkworth-Nanton are all scheduled to speak at the event. Joanna's mother, Diana Parkes, is also due to speak.

According to a representative for the Ministry of Justice, "This was an atrocious crime, and our sympathies are with Joanna Simpson's family and friends.

The deputy prime minister has promised to give this case his fullest personal attention and would use every legal tool at his disposal to keep the most dangerous criminals behind bars.

With their two young children were there, disgruntled aviator Brown bludgeoned Joanna, 46, to death in Ascot, Berkshire, in 2010. After that, he wrapped her corpse in plastic and put it in a previously dug grave in the Windsor Great Park's woods.

After being subjected to years of Brown's violence, harassment, and intimidation, Mrs. Simpson filed for divorce, and the two were now engaged in a court dispute over their money.

He was found not guilty of murder but was sentenced to 26 years in prison after pleading guilty to manslaughter on the basis of reduced culpability.

His upcoming release in November has Mrs. Simpson's family terrified.

According to a representative for the Joanna Simpson Foundation, "We are extremely glad that the Justice Secretary has agreed to meet with Joanna's family so that they may explain why they believe this case has gone so wrong."

We are sure that if Mr. Raab is given all the information, he would agree

with us that everything must be done
to stop the release of Robert Brown.

CHAPTER 4

Supporters and relatives will call on Mr. Raab to use his authority to prevent Brown's release tomorrow, including Joanna's mother Diana Parkes.

During a rally, they will speak with Carrie Johnson, the wife of former Prime Minister Boris, former Solicitor General Sir Robert Buckland, and ex-Home Secretary Priti Patel.

The Parole Board approved the release of John Worboys in 2018, the black cab rapist.

Priti Patel and Robert Buckland, both ex-cabinet members, are pleading with the government to use laws they helped pass in the legislature to prevent the automatic release of a wife murderer.

Using provisions in the Police, Crime, Sentencing and Courts (PCSC) Act of 2022, Ms. Patel, the former home secretary, and Mr. Buckland, the former justice secretary, are urging ministers to send Robert Brown's case to the parole board.

In October 2010, as his kids hid inside their Ascot, Berkshire house, Brown fatally bludgeoned his estranged wife Joanna Simpson, 46, to death with a claw hammer. Simpson's remains was interred by Brown in a pre-existing grave in Windsor Great Park.

Former British Airlines pilot Brown was sentenced to 26 years in prison in May 2011 after pleading guilty to manslaughter with diminished culpability. In November, after serving half of his sentence, he is scheduled for parole.

After discovering that Brown will be classified as a "important public protection case," which means that he is seen to represent a very high risk of severe damage, Diana Parkes, Simpson's mother, appealed to Dominic Raab, the Justice Secretary, personally on Saturday to keep Brown in jail.

On Wednesday, Ms. Parkes will hold a reception in Parliament where Ms. Patel, Mr. Buckland, and Carrie Johnson, the wife of Boris Johnson, will urge Dominic Raab to use his "authority to detain" Brown.

The PCSC Act 2022's section 132 gives Mr. Raab the authority to "submit high-risk offenders to the Parole Board in lieu of automatic release," so that is one option he has.

The Government should be where the rules and regulations are already in place, according to Ms. Patel, if anybody in the government is unsure.

"The Justice Secretary is able to change automatic regulations into scrutineering rules thanks to the additional powers provided by the PCSC Act," said Mr. Buckland. It should be taken into account and perhaps utilised, in my opinion.

The Joanna Simpson Foundation, a nonprofit that Parkes assisted in founding and which has been working to "change the care, support, and protection of children impacted by domestic violence and murder," has organized the event.

Once Mr. Raab consented to see the family, the celebration at Westminster Chapel would take place three days later. According to reports, Hetti Barkworth-Nanton, the co-founder of the organisation, will see Damian Hinds, the prisons minister, within the next week.

According to the Ministry of Justice, Mr. Raab "will do all in his power to keep the most dangerous criminals behind bars and has committed to give this case his closest personal attention."

With significant concerns were expressed about the probation department, Brown was classified as presenting a substantial danger of harm and needing close monitoring.

When violent misogynist Jordan McSweeney was released from jail and went on to kill law graduate Zara Aleena in Ilford, east London, in June 2022, governments and the service were accused of having "blood on their hands" last month.

The Joanna Simpson Foundation, established by her family to raise awareness about domestic violence, said in a statement on Sunday: "We are extremely delighted the Justice Secretary has agreed to meet with Joanna's family so they can explain in their own words what they believe has gone so wrong in this instance.

We are certain that Mr. Raab will agree with us that all necessary steps must be done to prevent the release of Robert Brown after he has been supplied with all the information.

When Brown arrived to deliver his children to their Ascot, Berkshire, home, he had concealed the hammer in one of their bags.

Before placing her corpse in his vehicle and burying her in Windsor Great Park, he struck his wife 14 times in the head with a hammer.

He was judged not guilty of murder but convicted of manslaughter in 2011 and given a sentence of 24 years for the death and an additional two years for hindering a coroner at Reading Crown Court.

Printed in Great Britain
by Amazon

23436940R10020